Hearts Linked by Courage

Real-life stories of challenge, triumph, and hope

CANADIAN MENTAL HEALTH ASSOCIATION
YORK AND SOUTH SIMCOE

IC PUBLISHING

Library and Archives Canada

Hearts Linked by Courage – Real-life stories of challenge, triumph, and hope
    Canadian Mental Health Association York and South Simcoe

Issued in print and electronic formats
ISBN (paperback): 978-1-927952-50-4
ISBN (PDF): 978-1-927952-51-1

Publishing: I C Publishing
Production: WeMakeBooks.ca

Printed in Canada
ICpublishing.ca

A NEW BUTTERFLY

By Stephen Marcus

Parents formed my vulnerable childhood with abuse;
no freedom or flight for me in my colourless world.
I was not a beautiful butterfly, but a small dull moth.
So that's what it was like to be a child.

Now I sit quietly and watch my granddaughter play.
She feels safe and secure to be whoever she wants to be.
I hear her speak her mind and express herself quite well.
So that is what it is like to be a child.

Her personality is bright, colourful, engaging, and gentle;
open to laugh, cry, and express feelings in her unique way,
without any apparent sense of limitations and boundaries.
So that is what it is like to be a child.

I have seen in her growth and joy that comes from learning;
love is expressed affectionately for all those close to her.
She soars in beauty and flies freely like an exquisite butterfly.
So that is what it is like to be a child.

Now I'm like a butterfly, transforming through many stages,
re-entering the world from my varying points of growth.
No longer am I that moth, but an unencumbered butterfly set free.
So that is what it's really like to be a child.

CONTENTS

PREFACE

*M*ental health issues have been with us since the beginning of time. We have witnessed a painfully slow, but nonetheless steady transformation in how we as individuals and a society have dealt with these issues. I would like to think that, in the 21st Century, we would have taken the spectre of mental health and mental illness out of the basement so to speak, and given the myriad of people who deal with mental health issues their rightful place in the world. The storytellers in this book continue their fight for that rightful place on an ongoing basis every day of their lives.

COURAGE, PERSEVERANCE, HOPE, TENACITY, STRENGTH

These are some of the words you will say to yourself when you read each story in this book. You'll come away knowing that the storytellers, and their journeys, are also a very important work in progress. A work in progress that will remain strong no matter what adversities they face.

This book has a purpose; to show you the reader that these storytellers' lives matter. I truly believe that when you read about their lives you will realize how incredible these people are. Their stories will move you, and make you think. They will take you on journeys you never thought possible. Their stories were not easy to write; they will introduce you to a world that is full of contradictions, deep pain, and triumph over that pain, and most importantly, full of life.

I have had the honour and the privilege of being in the company of my fellow storytellers. Their warmth, kindness, caring, and compassion have lifted me, and more significantly, provided me a safe place, and a community I can depend on. We all need to feel this. Welcome, dear reader, to our community.

— Randee Korman

FOREWORD

I have worked and lived in the mental health field for thirty-five years. It is paradoxical, exhilarating, and disheartening, that there is one critical aspect of mental wellbeing that has both changed the most, while at the same time changed the least. It is stigma!

What is immensely encouraging is that there is far more dialogue and discourse about mental illness than ever before. Further, as the floodgate of increased acceptance has opened, the rate at which further gains are made seems to be exponential. I am convinced that this great progress is not driven by the media and various campaigns by organizations to get the word out. It has been, and always will be, the people with lived experience — those who have the courage and conviction to tell all they can, that they are not their mental illness, that they are equals in ability.

Fittingly then, the impetus for this book came from the Speakers' Bureau at the Canadian Mental Health

Association York and South Simcoe. This diverse group, comprised of CMHA volunteers, are connected through their passion to strive to share their success and educate and inspire others to embark on their own recovery journey. Over the last six years they have delivered extensive presentations, led numerous discussions, and answered an immeasurable number of questions. The credo for the Speakers' Bureau is:

Raising Awareness – Reducing Stigma – Inspiring Hope ... And they certainly have!

To persevere in fighting the battle against stigma is central to all that the Speakers' Bureau is and does. This book holds their stories of struggle and triumph. They have been crafted with great thought for you to shed any remnants of stigma you may hold and to see the reality of recovery. Then, as you embrace this new-found hope you can, with compassion, offer support wherever needed. Consider starting with the most important person, yourself.

— Neil Howard
Director of Programs
CMHA York and South Simcoe

Prose

CREATED FOR JOY
By Michael Finnerty

If life made no room for mistakes or trial and error,
I wouldn't be here today.

When you think of mental illness, I bet the word joy doesn't come to your mind. This is what I thought was lacking in my life prior to being diagnosed with a mental illness.

While at Trent University, I was drawn to learn how to meditate. I began to believe that my identity was founded in any culture other than the one into which I was born. I was living off campus and one day happened to make my way into a New Age book store. I wasn't into New Age; in fact the previous year I had become a born-again Christian. On this particular day though, what caught my attention was a book by one of the founders of yoga in the United States in the 1920s,

Paramahansa Yoganada. I in no way want to say anything negative about yoga and meditation; however, if I had heeded my younger brother's advice when he discovered I was reading this book on meditation, I wouldn't have dropped out of university and left it all to become a yogi.

I had been living in a rented room in a house with a bunch of guys, and never thought of myself as a spiritual person. The book's content had a profound impact on me though, and my mind was set. I was going to a Christian and Hindu monastery called an ashram, and no one could convince me otherwise, not even my friend who told me she could see auras, significant signs or appearances that New Agers often talked about.

I did attend college after high school before getting involved in the environmental movement in 1995, studied musical theatre performance, and then focused on becoming a full time yogi. The transformation was complete.

The next few years I spent working at different jobs, after moving back home for a period of time to save money, but still the joy in my life was coming from my spirituality. About twice a week I would drive myself to a meditation group in Toronto, Ontario, until signs of mental illness started appearing in my life. I remember sitting up in my bed one afternoon, enjoying the calmness my mind experienced as I was meditating, and it seemed like something dropped in my consciousness. One night I really felt a change in my mood as I was driving to Toronto for meditation, and could feel a weakness in my hands as I was holding the steering wheel. Following the meditation I felt really sleepy.

Not too long afterward, I found myself at Markham Stouffville Hospital being admitted voluntarily into the mental health unit. By the way, looking back I think it was the best thing that ever happened to me.

With all the meditation I was doing, I had begun to neglect my body. What drove me to the hospital? I stopped eating three meals a day and would spend the entire day meditating. I don't believe that meditation is bad for you, but somehow for me it proved to be an obsession that I couldn't control. In actual fact, I'm sure the right kind of meditation can be very healing for some people suffering from mental illness, and part of my recovery right now involves a form of meditation that promotes awareness. Meditation shouldn't be mindless, but mindful, and the choice to incorporate a form of this in my daily life keeps my mood in control.

Eventually, my association with a Christian church was instrumental in shedding positive light on my path and my purpose. The family that I have gained from my church has saved me from very desperate thoughts at times, and in 2007, I was baptized into the faith. In spite of my low self esteem, they accepted and recognized me for who I was.

I am not saying religion is the answer to recovery, but expressing myself through activities that make me aware I have a soul sure help me immensely. If I was to look back now at my choice to leave university and become a yogi, I would say that it was a good choice. It was part of my growing up.

If life made no room for mistakes or trial and error, I wouldn't be here today. From my variety of experiences, I would love to facilitate conversations in faith communities, and elsewhere, bringing awareness and compassion to where people hiding with mental illness can be fully accepted and integrated into their respective communities and exist in our country as people with a voice. I would like to see a general acceptance of those who are suffering from any kind of emotional distress to be able to talk about it freely in their families, churches, mosques, synagogues, temples, etc.

Looking ahead then, it makes sense for me to set some goals. My first is family-oriented, to become more inclusive with them regarding my treatment process. Knowledge will make them better equipped to travel this road with me. Secondly, over the coming years, I will aim to give my community a better understanding of poverty and the challenges it provides for people with mental illness.

If there is a secret to recovery, number one is pretty fundamental: if you are suffering from a mental illness, you need to take your meds and listen to your doctor. The next secret is to be you. For me, it was first as a student, then as a meditative person, and now I am back to being me, someone who culminates all these aspects of my journey. When you accept your illness and accept yourself, you may find life a little easier, and you just might discover joy again, or for the very first time.

WORK IN PROGRESS
By Craig Stevenson

Today, I'm happy to say that I
have never felt better about myself.

It was October 2010, and thinking I was having a
heart attack, I checked myself into our local hospital
emergency department.

The past five years had been extremely stressful. In
2005, my father was diagnosed with cancer and died,
leaving me despondent and depressed. In 2009 my
brother almost died when he was hit by a car, and that
same year, mother died of cancer too. Finally, in 2010,
evicted from the townhouse I'd been living in with my
family for the past ten years, I had to move into a trailer.
I felt like a failure, abandoned and alone. Ultimately, it
was necessary to move from that trailer to a shelter with
my wife and daughter, and subsequently, I needed to

apply for social assistance. Concerned about what my daughter would think about me, I felt even more dejected. My grief led me along a tumultuous path, and the loss of loved ones and a safe, secure home took its toll.

Life hadn't started out that way. I'd had a fairly normal and happy childhood. At age twenty-six, I married, and my wife and I raised three children. I had experienced some difficulty with drugs and alcohol, (starting with drinking and smoking cigarettes and cannabis at just fifteen), but in 1994, with the miracle of an alcohol-allergic reaction, I was sober.

Still the challenges continued, for there I lay in the hospital for eight days, sleeping for the first three days without being sedated. I was told that I'd experienced a panic attack and psychosis, likely amplified by my repeated substance abuse. Leaving the hospital with the suggestion of signing up for Addition Services of York Region for my marijuana addiction, I graduated a few months later, clean. In the new year I attempted to return to work, starting with a large trade show. With "all" riding on the success of this show, I was experiencing intense anxiety. My doctor at the time gave me a prescription for a sedative to be taken three times daily, and I ended up back in bed, this time at home for seven months!

Hopeless, feeling useless, and abusing the medication, I was suddenly denied a refill for my sedative. The withdrawal from my medications caused me to become suicidal, and once again, I checked myself into the hospital; this time I was diagnosed as having bipolar disorder.

Upon discharge in August 2011, I was presented with the following recommendations:

- Join a 12-Step support group.
- Participate in the day program at Southlake Hospital.
- Get personal counseling.
- Take all the medication the psychiatrist prescribes ... even when feeling better!
- Apply for ODSP with help of the hospital social worker.
- Link up with a CMHA case management worker.

This is when my recovery truly began. I surrendered and decided that the choices I had made to date were what got me to where I was! So, if I did everything *they* told me to do, and it didn't work, then it would all be *their* fault!

After being placed on the CMHA waiting list for a case manager (well worth the wait, I must admit), I met with my worker who said that, while we needed to get to know each other better, for now he wanted to focus on my immediate needs. The worker asked whether that was finances, my fears, housing, or something else. I couldn't emphasize enough that housing was my major concern, and recall the worker saying, "Leave it with me. I'll get back to you at the meeting next week."

True to his word, at our second meeting, my worker offered me a spot in the CMHA Housing Program and I was able to move into a three-bedroom apartment. The combined resources and devoted efforts of my case manager, Alcoholics Anonymous (AA), and my sponsor enabled me to start my life anew.

Today, I'm happy to say that I have never felt better about myself. Previously, my priorities were set as follows: a) spirituality, b) family, and c) mental health and addictions.

Now I have refined it accordingly: a) spirituality, b) mental health and addictions, and c) family. Mental health has to come before family, because if I lose my mental health again, I will be no good for anybody, or anything!

And I have a recovery prescription for myself:
- Follow all of my mentors' advice!
- Give back to the people and organizations that have helped me on my journey of recovery and continue to do so. (I credit my wife for being the most awesome and supportive person ever.)
- Thank the "God of my Understanding" every single day, for the second and third chances given to me!

I have enrolled in the PREFER Course, to become a trained Peer Support Worker in the hope of pursuing employment in the addiction and/or mental health field in the near future. Further, I sincerely look forward to the possibility of working with like-minded people to become an effective influence in my community and the world.

In addition to participating in CMHA's Speakers' Bureau, it's an honour to tell my recovery story monthly at the mental health program at Southlake Regional Health Centre (Newmarket Ontario) and also at the Stepping Stones Mental Health Day Hospital located at Mackenzie Health.

I'm proudly a work-in-progress. Now I share my story to let others know that there is hope.

THE CHILD WITHIN
By Dom Polito

I took a journey to learn about what had
come over me. I read books, meditated, did yoga …

*D*are I listen?
I remember riding my bike, swimming in the pool,
playing with my friends, and always being with family.
We all had a precious innocence growing up, and it was
a time full of memories I've never forgotten.

In my teens, I became the object of bullying, like
most kids of a different ethnic background. I recall
vividly, being dragged by my hair across a football field,
and being sucker punched just walking by someone.
I've been stigmatized about the length of my hair my
whole life, and it still happens even today. On another
occasion, I rode to the library on the brand new bike
my dad had bought me, just to return my books. I

parked it with all the other bikes, and proceeded inside. Moments later, I came back only to find that my bike was gone, forever.

Did it affect me? Of course it did. It made me withdraw from people and eventually, the school system as well. I discovered music at the time and took a liking to it, and that's all I ever looked forward to. It was my therapy. I remember skipping school and going down to the ravine on a sunny day. What a serene place. I would just sit and play. That was my happy place.

Abruptly and unexpectedly, my dad had a stroke at forty-four years young, followed by several heart attacks. I knew what was going on, but I don't think I fully understood. It was tough to see my dad like that. I guess I never realized that we could have lost him very easily. All of a sudden, my mom was the only one working and we were in trouble. When my brother finished school he began working where my dad had been employed. I finally got a job as well, and when I reflect on it now, it was my way out.

Life's hard knocks didn't stop there though. When I was eighteen years of age, an industrial accident on a faulty piece of machinery amputated half of my index and middle fingers. This completely changed my whole life. I didn't realize until much later that I had actually suffered severe PTSD as well. All I could think about at the time was that I was never going to play guitar again. This was the start of a scary downward direction for me, as I spiraled into depression. Fueled by anger, resentment, anxiety, sadness, and fear, the next three years were spent struggling with these emotions and feeling sorry for myself.

Eventually, I came to the conclusion that I had to attempt playing guitar again or move on to something else. Cut from the cloth where I was taught to grin and bear it, that's what I did. So I chose guitar and started from scratch. Anything I'd learned in previous years was gone; I devised a way to make it work, but it wasn't easy. Nevertheless, I went through life this way and managed for quite some time.

Then, in 1996, out of the blue, I started experiencing full blown panic attacks and major anxiety. My life was productively jam packed, with a full-time day job and playing in not one, but three bands. However, during a performance in Toronto one day, I took a bathroom break—I couldn't figure out what was happening. I barely made it through the show. And the very next day, everything came to a screeching halt. I became confined to my home, riddled with fear and agoraphobia. This anxiety disorder was crippling. For the next three years of my life, I merely existed, unable to work or be part of the bands.

It took quite a while, but over the next seven or eight years I took a journey to learn about what had come over me. I read books, watched videos, meditated, did yoga, went to the gym three times a week, saw therapists, and tried to determine a way to make my life manageable again. It was definitely a rollercoaster ride, and I seemed to have it under control for so long.

In 2015 though, it hit me like a ton of bricks once more, and stopped me in my tracks just like before. Why was this happening? I had this down pat now, right? I guess not. After thirty years, panic attacks and anxiety were back in full swing and not even meds were helping.

It escalated to having attacks of hyperventilating for up to an eight-hour period. I didn't even know that it was possible to lay in bed unable to catch my breath for hours at a time. My family doctor advised me to get on a waiting list for an anxiety group class, which I did, and thankfully I was eventually accepted into the program.

This was the beginning of a new chapter, the critical turning point. I've been involved in many different programs and drop-in centres, and through this and volunteering, have learned some valuable lessons. The Stepping Stones Program at Mackenzie Health encouraged me to delve deeply into mental health. In my mind I always felt I had a gift to help people. I imagined that would happen when I retired, but it seems to have come around much sooner, and I'm embracing it full on. People resonate with me. I am in the right place.

Through this experience, I am working toward becoming an advocate for mental health. This comes with absolutely no resistance; it chooses me. Volunteering with the CMHA Speakers' Bureau and their Choices Program, as well as completing training to obtain numerous certificates, has finally secured me a position with CMHA as a Peer Support Specialist with their Housing First Program.

I haven't been on this road alone. I'm married, have a lovely wife, two daughters, and three grandkids, and am also a professional musician touring and performing all over North America. It's a busy life that I do my best to balance so that my relationships are properly nurtured.

My family is the most important thing in my life, and I need to make time for them. I know that work will always be there, so I need to allocate time for family. I believe that means caring for me as well, and have come to realize how very important my own self-care really is.

The people I have met in the mental health field, including the social workers at Mackenzie Health, are incredible. And the folks I have met suffering with various mental health issues always take to me—we speak the same language. I plan to help remove the mental health stigma, and perhaps it'll mean incorporating my love of music to accomplish this. I would certainly welcome that!

My involvement now, in mental health, helps others and also helps me at the same time. In hindsight, I think I may have already had some of the answers along the way. All I had to do was listen carefully within.

FOOTPRINTS ON MY HEART
By Liz Hall

Forgiveness wasn't forgetting or condoning
the acts of others; it was an act of will
that allowed me to move forward.

*D*id you ever wrap your arms around yourself just
to imagine someone else hugging you? Did you
ever feel strange, foreign, and singled out by everyone?
Did you ever get laughed at and didn't know why? Did
you ever hide your sensitivity and your true feelings for
fear of being reprimanded? I did. It's part of my journey
through depression, anxiety, and borderline personality
disorder (BPD).

There is no universal account of mental illness; that's
why it's so hard to diagnose and part of the reason so
many people tend to pass judgement. My story is of my
illness, my fight to live, and my will to survive. For as

long as my memory serves me, I've felt I didn't belong and that I was very different. An abundance of somewhat normal childhood emotions seemed to plague me. I was easily hurt and lived in constant fear of being criticized, humiliated, and rejected. I would go through many lonely days and nights wishing I'd never been born.

When I was nine years old, I began to suffer from intense emotional pain, feelings of emptiness, and obsessive compulsive behaviour, which just happened to be the year my dad moved on to start over with a new family. It began with uncontrollable eating. I realized that food gave me comfort when I was hurt or angry, and the more I ate the better I felt. I would steal and hoard food in desperation, and convinced myself that food was love and I couldn't get enough of it. As I grew into a teenager, my destructive eating habits intensified, resulting in an eating disorder where I would overeat and purge, or starve to punish myself for my weakness. By the time I reached fourteen, I had experimented with cigarettes, drugs, and alcohol, as they took away the pain, even if just temporarily, and these became my only friends. My existence consisted of a combination of destructive eating and dangerous alcohol and drug abuse, always indulged in isolation.

By this time I had convinced myself it was my fault that others treated me as they did. I wasn't strong or smart enough to avoid the constant hurtful actions and behaviours of those around me and became more isolated and lonely. I was withdrawn, suspicious, and entirely uncommunicative with my parents and got agitated quickly. At the least little altercation, I felt threatened. The year I turned eighteen, I began to harm myself, which seemed yet another form of punishment for my limitations … the cutting released a torrent of resentment and hurt.

Shortly after I graduated high school, I tried to start a new life and took a permanent job out of town where no one knew me. I became a people pleaser, wanting everyone to like me. Paranoid that I was incapable of functioning in a work environment or was likely to make multiple mistakes, I struggled. I was experiencing memory problems, missing appointments, maxing credit cards, and forgetting work deadlines. You see, I had next to no life skills and was suffering from chronic stress, compounded by physical ailments and burnout. I never spoke to anyone about my feelings of despair and how close I was coming to ending my life. When it was suggested I try to get help, that wasn't an option I was willing to explore, at least initially, since I knew no other way of living.

There were a few times throughout my twenties when I did think about reaching out. I had met my future husband at this point and he encouraged me to see a doctor. Diagnosed with bulimia/anorexia and mild depression at twenty-five, I was admitted to an out-patient clinic and prescribed a mild antidepressant. What I thought I needed was a quick guarantee that this treatment would work and my life would change for the better. However, I was experiencing uncomfortable side effects from the meds and not feeling any better, so I lost confidence in the health care system, stopped taking the medication, quit the outpatient clinic, and continued along my destructive path. Many years would pass before I saw another doctor.

The year I turned forty, I thought it was time to find a family physician. Upon examining my past medical records, this doctor suggested I be tested for mental illness. I became very agitated and adamantly refused, believing I had tried to put my past behind me and had acquaintances who I felt would be mortified if they thought I had any kind of illness. My unpleasant memories of clinics, medication, and being labelled still haunted me, so I wanted nothing to do with his ideas.

Unfortunately, each year that went by saw the darkness of my mood and outlook on life increase. It was obvious my employer was concerned about my behaviour, as I was taking numerous days off due to physical ailments and mental anxiety, resulting in several panic attacks throughout the day. Any social interaction was avoided at all cost. I always felt like I was on a roller coaster with my emotions going up and down at the drop of a hat. Last, but not least, my marriage was falling apart, as I was lashing out at my husband, and pushing him out of my life.

On June 30, 2011 at the age of forty-eight, my life changed. I quit my job with no thought of how I was going to live and carry on, and revisited thoughts of ending it all. The only person I wanted to see was my doctor. I didn't know it then, but he had never given up on me. He took one look at me and called the EMS. I was admitted to the inpatient mental health ward at the hospital and the person I'd known was about to begin her transformation. The week I spent as an inpatient in the hospital was surreal. For the first time in my life I felt safe, protected, and that maybe I was going to be okay. The doctors and nurses were kind, sympathetic, and didn't judge me for my mistakes or past behaviour. In reality, I didn't want to leave this feeling of being so cared for.

It took a lot of trial and error and patience to find the right combination of meds. I was prescribed an antipsychotic, mood stabilizer, and antidepressant, and my moods started to stabilize. It was hard not to give into self-pity. I was having difficulty absorbing the fact that I had a chronic illness and that I had to take meds for the rest of my life. It wasn't until I realized it was up to me to get my moods stabilized, and that there was no magic cure, that I began to turn the corner on the road to recovery. Letting go of the old patterns was my choice, but acceptance of my diagnosis and moving on was the most challenging thing I had ever done. My life had been wrapped up in decades of harmful behaviour, but with the help of CMHA, I was able to go forward.

I was enrolled in group therapy as an outpatient. This offered me a haven. I knew I was safe and I was around others recovering who didn't judge me. I didn't feel so alone anymore. Previously, I had lived in constant fear of being bullied, humiliated, and rejected. It wasn't until I was diagnosed and finally met others who were also struggling that I felt I actually fit in somewhere and was normal. I was encouraged to acknowledge my anger and fear, and taught by counsellors and nurses to express feelings through art, music, and journaling, and through journaling I discovered a lot of painful memories were alleviated.

Dieticians and pharmacists educated us on how our meds worked, what side effects to expect, and why unhealthy eating and lifestyle choices can adversely influence brain chemistry and promote mood episodes. It was explained to me that depression is indisputably biochemical and no amount of medical tests can confirm a diagnosis—instead psychiatrists rely on a list of nine indicators devised more than a hundred years ago. In my case, I had met every one of those nine symptoms.

One mental health nurse left footprints on my heart, coming into my life just when I needed her. She provided me with guidance, support, and a strong shoulder to cry on. She taught me to forgive myself for the wrong choices I had made in the past. She also showed me that forgiveness wasn't forgetting or condoning the acts of others, but was an act of will that allowed me to move forward and not to be victimized again.

Living with BPD is a lifelong challenge. It's hard to predict when a mood episode will come, how long it will last, and how severe it will be; it's an ongoing process of maintaining optimism. I still struggle with my anxiety and social phobias, but I now acknowledge it's my responsibility to overcome my obstacles and turn negatives into positives. I now have the courage to take chances, and if I falter, I am able to pick myself up and keep going. I do experience mild side effects such as headaches and fine hand tremors, but the medication by far exceeds my expectations, and my most profound need is peace of mind.

Healing involves moving backwards sometimes. It doesn't happen immediately, and once in a while, I wake up and don't have the energy to be happy or stay healthy that day, but I am moving forward one step at a time. I know I cannot be loved, appreciated, or have the approval of everyone; I also know my illness is not my fault, nor did it make me weak or a failure.

I need to concentrate on being myself, managing my emotions, and recognizing potential triggers. I can take constructive criticism without feeling I am being ridiculed or verbally attacked. I do encounter my neediness, my pain of abandonment, and my invisible scars, but I have also realized my sensitivity is my strength. It means I am okay. I have learned to listen to my feelings, not push them away, accept my emotions, respect myself, and set boundaries.

Hurtful phrases like, "She's lost her marbles" or "She's loony, crazy, or nuts" were directed at me constantly. It's easy to throw terms such as these around in casual conversation, but doing so promotes mental health stigma. Mental illness is a serious sickness you cannot see and is not the person's fault. Only a few decades ago, many people with severe depression and other mental disorders were shunned, placed in strait-jackets, and locked away in institutions. And while society has come a long way since then, we still have improvements to make in terms of getting people the assistance they need while treating them with dignity and respect. Choose your words with care and compassion.

There have been great strides made in this area through associations that try to dispel stigma. CARE is one of those organizations. The word CARE stands for Compassion, Advocacy, Recognition, and Education. CARE is used in support workshops across Canada and the USA, promoting compassion, alleviating stigma, eliminating isolation, and most importantly, educating and emphasizing to the public that our illness is not a sign of weakness or a lack of self control. A key human need is to have a sense of belonging and awareness that you are loved, and CARE is helping to accomplish this.

I still live and struggle with an ache for relationships I will never have, but through the positive actions and support of others, I am encouraged to tell my story. I joined the Speakers' Bureau of CMHA with the hope that I would touch someone who might still be struggling and let them know they are not alone. As well, I volunteer weekly at a community women's support group for those dealing with mental health issues. This is my way of giving back to the community that has supported me.

More days than not, I live simply and well, with the support of my doctor who was always there for me, my husband who stood by me through thick and thin, and of course my special nurse with whom I still keep in touch. I invest more time and energy into my mental health than any other aspect of my life because without a stable mind, I risk losing everything important to me. I believe that as a result of my diagnosis and continuing journey, I now care more deeply, appreciate life and laugh more, and yes cry when I need to without feeling guilty. Thanks to organizations such as CMHA, I don't suffer in silence anymore.

HOPE, HUMOUR, AND HAPPINESS:
A PATH TOWARD RECOVERY
By Nyk Morrigan

Rather than fear or judge what we don't understand,

let's be open ...

My journey of recovery along the path toward mental health is a personal and vulnerable one, yet honest and forthright. I'm not intending to evoke pity or sorrow about the difficulties that inevitably arose. My goal is to provide a sense of hope, both for those living with a diagnosis and those supporting loved ones, and ultimately to open up dialogue about what living with mental illness looks like. My wish is that it will shift how you personally think about the words mental health in order to initiate discussion amongst co-workers, family, and friends to create a more positive understanding.

What does it actually mean to be mentally healthy anyway? According to the Mental Health Commission of Canada Report 2012, mental health is described as the capacity for all of us to feel, think, and act in ways that enhance our ability to enjoy life and deal with the challenges we face. It's a positive sense of emotional and spiritual wellbeing that respects many things; most importantly, personal dignity. Unlike many other definitions, this reflects something more positive. Mental health is frequently assumed to be the absence of a diagnosis. This is the framework that I hope to challenge as I tell to you about my story.

My journey begins in childhood, as everyone's does. I grew up in a rural town, the youngest of five. The first daughter was born before my parents were married. She was given up for adoption and her existence became the family secret. When I look back, I can see now that my parents were a product of their own unhealthy childhoods. They used ineffective strategies to cope with and hide a huge family secret for many years. One parent turned to alcohol to cope, an unhealthy pattern deep within our Irish roots. The other parent drew from an unhealthy interpretation of religion to escape the pain. I was raised with the understanding that burying your emotions and resorting to addictive behaviours was the way to deal with life's challenges. However, I feel it's important to highlight the effective strategies I was taught in order to get through difficult times; skills like humour, compassion, and gratitude.

Throughout my life, I have lived with high levels of stress and anxiety. I've received help to better understand why the same negative patterns kept resurfacing in my life. Surely, there was more to it than my misguided coping strategies. I've been diagnosed with Attention-Deficit/Hyperactivity Disorder (ADHD), Generalized Anxiety Disorder (GAD), Borderline Personality Disorder (BPD) and even Obsessive Compulsive Disorder (OCD) … and if I had come out thirty years ago, my Lesbian, Gay, Bisexual, Transgender (LGBT) identity would have become another clinical label. Just to be clear, I'm not intending to dismiss or make light of being diagnosed. What I am hoping to do is present a new way of looking at it. In my experience, people can get stuck on labels when it comes to this topic. Instead of seeing diagnosis as a static part of one's identity, (which stigmatizes people), *maybe* we could view it through the lens of something more fluid and changing (in hopes of removing stigma)?

In high school, I volunteered as a peer helper, then as a young adult began my career in personal support work. I started off providing care for people with physical disabilities, then became an educational assistant for autistic kids, and moved on to work as a behavioural councillor. My career has been about advocating for people who have been disenfranchised and raising awareness about how we can respect personal dignity and self-autonomy. I will be the first to admit that, as a caregiver, I thought I knew how challenging it gets receiving care. However, it wasn't until I faced my own mental health break and became totally dependent on the system that I truly understood the stigma that comes with being diagnosed.

After a series of abusive dynamics, I found myself in a place of total desperation and attempted to take my own life. I went into a forest and took enough medication to render me unconscious for a total of five days. Miraculously, I woke up, *on my own*. I was in a complete daze and had no idea how much time had passed; however, I knew it was essential to find help. Unbeknownst to me, during those five days outside, I ended up with severe frostbite that caused permanent nerve damage in my feet. I managed to get to a nearby bike path and once there, a passerby recognized me from the "missing" posters. I was immediately rushed to hospital and remained there for the next month.

The next year of my life would prove to be both enlightening and transformative. Due to the circumstances surrounding my discharge, I was in need of full care and an accessible home. I was lucky to have family close by who were able to take me in and support me on my journey of healing. It was during this time that I realized how difficult and frustrating it is to advocate for oneself and the systemic challenges people face while trying to access care.

In an environment of stigma and judgment, it also takes a lot of courage to advocate for oneself. I had to face a lot of my own preconceived ideas about what it meant to be diagnosed, as well as the judgments of others. Only after I started being involved in my community again did I realize how significant the stigma of mental illness really is. Many close friends and acquaintances reached out to me in search of some kind of hope because their family members or close friends were going through something similar. There was a desperate attempt to find answers and speak to someone who wouldn't judge them. I commonly heard sighs of relief as people said, "It's so nice to speak to someone who gets it."

It was then I realized that my lived experience could actually be seen as a gift rather than a curse. This realization was the start of my involvement with the Canadian Mental Health Association (CMHA). I signed up for the Community Connections program and the staff supported me in developing a unique program called, Under the Rainbow, a support and social group for members of the Lesbian, Gay, Bisexual, Transgender, Two spirited, Queer (LGBTTQ) community; a community that also deals with stigma. From there, I continued volunteering in whatever capacity I was physically capable of, beginning with presenting to youth in schools, the staff at the internal conference, as well as doing talks for the Speakers' Bureau. I am proud to stay I now work for CMHA as a Peer Support Specialist. This gives me the privilege of supporting people from a lived experience perspective, an opportunity I feel so grateful for.

While my journey has moved in a positive direction, I recognize the privileges that have helped get me to the place I am now. Not every person has the support necessary or the access to resources in the way I did. So part of why I am sharing my story is to help give a voice to those who have not been given the opportunity. What I have noticed above all else is that so many of us feel shame in admitting that we have a diagnosis. The stigma of feeling less than whole or complete (whether self-imposed or imposed by others), is very debilitating. The fight to believe you are worth it while living in a world that so often tells us we are not, is exceptionally challenging and exhausting. Add to that a sense of hopelessness, a lack of support, and medications with negative side effects (things I am personally quite familiar with) ... the challenge becomes even greater.

How then does one find hope in what seems to be a hopeless situation? Let's reframe how we understand and perceive mental illness. I now dedicate much of my time to help raise awareness and encourage people to look at this from a different angle. If you look at a tree from one angle, you see one perspective, but the more you walk around it, the more angles you see. I have come to embrace my diagnosis. I look at it from a more positive perspective. While I don't want to discount the challenges, I also don't want to solely focus on them. I joke that if it wasn't for my OCD, I wouldn't have been as successful as I was being a personal organizer, or that my ADHD made me really skilled at hyper-focusing on tasks to get the job done well. Maybe the reason we can't *fix* mental illness is because we aren't meant to, and being different is actually a gift. Let me reiterate that I'm not discounting the challenges people face or the difficulties that arise. When things are most challenging, it is essential to take each day one day at a time, ask for support ('cause it does exist) *while* respecting people's personal dignity/choice, and remembering that every individual is unique and there is no quick solution or template for understanding a mental illness.

I hope my reflection provides some insight into how we can support our loved ones, how we can love ourselves, and how we can encourage ourselves and others to look outside the box for answers. I would love to see the stigma that is associated with mental illness lessen and our acceptance increase. My hope is that we learn to use a different lens to view mental health, and then allow the framework we employ to comprehend the challenges to fall more along a spectrum of understanding instead of an "us versus them" ideology. I believe once the stigma is removed, we can find more effective strategies to face these challenges together. Rather than fear or judge what we don't understand, let's be open to acquiring the knowledge necessary to move forward, equipped and ready to put a more positive face on mental health for future generations.

JUST ME
By Tali Kramer

Now I believe I can achieve anything …

*O*nce upon a time I entered this world as a fairly healthy newborn. This might sound slightly understated, but I feel like so much has happened between birth and now that I need to start at the beginning. I was just a regular child, or so it seemed. I went to school, did okay, played with my friends, dared my parents every now and then, and attempted all things that most normal children do.

It wasn't until I was twelve that the turmoil started in my life. I moved from Israel to South Africa with my parents and two younger siblings, had to learn a new language, and adapt to a totally new culture. I knew little English, and it certainly didn't help that I went to a Jewish school where the other kids discriminated against me simply because I was Israeli. I was either bullied or ignored. The only kids in my grade who accepted me were the few other Israelis, and another sweet boy who was a misfit simply because he lived in a Jewish orphanage. Desperate to feel good about myself, I devoted myself to my studies, hoping that I would do well. However, such was not the case, and I was devastated. I sunk into deep depression.

A year later, I moved to a regular public high school, hoping that would improve my detrimental self-esteem issues. As eager as I was though, to be accepted by my peers, I was immature, and did not know how to fit in. I had few friends, and did not have the social life that most teenagers crave. I became even more depressed and confused, and once more tried diligently to immerse myself into my studies.

This time, I graduated from a private high school with satisfactory grades, but quit university after about a year, and moved back to Israel at the age of twenty. There I enrolled in university only to drop out again after failing. I did not know what to do with myself, so I went through life aimlessly, searching for direction. Eventually I moved with my parents to New York where at last I successfully completed university with high grades. In spite of this, I wasn't happy. Although my depression was at bay, I was not leading the full life of a university student.

When I completed my degree, I moved to Canada, where my mental health issues started to interfere with my life. For a while I seemed relatively okay. I worked as a teacher and even tutored to supplement my income; I paid my bills; I was functional. However, after a while, when I was working as a supply teacher, signs of depression returned. I lost my appetite, and the little "joie de vivre" that I had. Suicidal thoughts plagued me, so I went to my family doctor who was very concerned, and prescribed an antidepressant. Luckily, it worked, and I was able to continue teaching and even did some tutoring. A few months later, I secured a full-time position as a Special Education teacher in a private school and did quite well until I started encountering some unwelcome symptoms—all the typical symptoms of bipolar disorder, type 2: when I wasn't depressed, I was hypomanic. I had racing thoughts, gambled online all night long, and lost a lot of my hard-earned money. I did not sleep much, and my speech was so rapid that it was almost blurred. I lost focus at work. When the academic year came to an end, many teachers were dismissed due to shortage of work, but in my case, I believe they just knew I had lost my ability to perform all my usual duties and that something was wrong.

Shortly beforehand, I had visited my family physician again, who made calls to psychiatrists right away. Fortunately, he found a wonderful psychiatrist who could see me that very same week and diagnosed me with bipolar mood disorder, type 2 rapid cycling. My journey with the pharmaceuticals began then and there. I'd be lying if I said that it wasn't trial and error, because it certainly was. While my psychiatrist and I were working hard to find the right combination of medications for me, I tried my hand at work once more, albeit unsuccessfully. I was emotional, still lacked focus, and felt like a failure. It did not help that I gained a lot of weight on the drug, Zyprexa, which made me feel extremely unattractive, especially considering the fact that I had always been very slim.

It was then I began to see that it was no shame for me to turn to the mental health system. The right combination of medications finally gave me the stability I'd been missing. With the help of my psychiatrist, I applied to the Ontario Disability Support Program (ODSP) and was placed on the program promptly. I also applied for case management and within a year, a case manager from Crosslinks was assigned to me.

Now I live independently in a Crosslinks apartment, along with my wonderful, sweet dog. As well, I volunteer with Canadian Mental Health Association (CMHA) York Region and South Simcoe, and have a great support system that includes my psychiatrist, case manager, parents, and a few good friends. I'm also planning on re-entering the work force in the near future. I owe a debt of gratitude to CMHA, Crosslinks, and my parents, for helping me to return to a new normal … a life full of possibilities.

Yes, I still have my challenges, but overall I realize that I've come a long way! Now, I believe I can achieve anything, and have the strength to accomplish whatever goals I may set for myself.

MY UNIQUE GIFT
By *Julie Tran*

After facing them, our obstacles actually
help create who we are... stronger, more resilient.

With having learning disabilities all my life, I have struggled and faced many barriers. In my childhood and teenager years, I experienced emotional bullying, was teased, underestimated, and discouraged by teachers and classmates alike.

One night before my grade eight graduation ceremony, my grandpa passed away. I was devastated and felt his loss deeply. We had always been very close; only he seemed to understand me, and he trusted me. Now he was gone and I felt alone.

As I came of age, I went to work, something most people eagerly anticipate. However, at the bank where I was employed, I was harassed by co-workers without provocation, and eventually dismissed. I had done nothing wrong, but a supervisor's incriminating statement was all it took. It seemed as though my appearance was judged in a discriminatory manner with no true assessment of what I could actually accomplish. After this incident, I couldn't handle anymore. I had reached a breaking point, and in 2009, attempted my first suicide by overdosing with an entire bottle of pills.

Life became even more difficult and I continued bumping into more obstacles that only succeeded in increasing my stress levels. The pressures wore me down until I was so depressed that I started to think there was no sense living in this world; I felt so useless. On numerous occasions, I attempted suicide, due to the negativity that swamped me. During this complex period, I never felt there was anyone to encourage me to go to the hospital and seek the help I so desperately needed.

In 2011, after having a syncope episode, I started to lose my vision. The emergency doctor suspected this temporary loss of consciousness was caused by a seizure; it was certainly a scary experience. Meanwhile, with major depression and anxiety, I began to hear voices as well. This was combined with a neurological disorder which to this date still has not been clinically defined.

Someone once said that with all my disabilities, "You might only get a janitor's job," or even worse, "You'll end up living on the street."

I was first hospitalized in 2013, albeit begrudgingly, for fear that people might view and treat me differently … a common reaction to the unknown. Then, in 2014, a concerned counselor at my school made the call to have me admitted again; because of my history, I was a higher risk to attempt suicide. The voices I heard had increased to the stage I couldn't control them. However, after being hospitalized twice, I felt much better. Soon I learned that no matter how difficult life may seem, ending it was not the solution; in fact, facing it and showing people who I really was helped turn things around. It was important to be strong and not to listen to those who tended to underestimate and discourage because they might not understand. My psychiatrist and Accessible Coach helped me greatly to see the real value of my life.

As a result, life started to change for the better afterward; my family is now more understanding and supportive, and presently I only take minimal medications to stabilize the depression, anxiety, and psychosis. Upon reflecting back on being told I'd never get a job or be able to survive in this world, I feel confident about what I've been able to accomplish, including attending college in Oshawa where I've met three wonderful friends.

Actually I still have learning disabilities, mental health illnesses, and a neurological disorder, but my vision has been restored by taking some natural remedies. As well, I'm successful and self-supporting. I currently live in a rented condo, and am also volunteering in a development company in Markham and at the Y.M.C.A. It feels good to be able to show the doubters how I've risen above the adversity! Today, I would say, "Hey, I am alive, and I'm doing well." My ultimate dream is that one day I will open up a store of my own, both either online or in the community.

From all of my experiences, I'd like to share a couple of things that I've learned. First, try to view mental health or other disabilities as unique gifts, not disorders. After facing them, our obstacles actually help create who we are. Eventually, you will become stronger and more resilient.

Then no matter what difficulty you may encounter, keep a positive outlook. For example, if you hear voices or see things telling you to harm yourself, take control, and take action. Connect with the supportive people and groups in your life, Journey safe and journey strong. Say an emphatic "No" to those things in life that are detrimental to you and weigh you down.

Remember, ending your life is not a solution! Staying alive is!! You are special, one-of-a-kind, so don't be afraid to get the help you need. Welcome help, and embrace life!

Now that you've read my story, it's my hope you will see the person I've become. Right now I am strong, I live independently, listen only to the positive voices, and continue to volunteer. If I can deal with all my negativity and overcome it, I believe you will be able to do so too, whatever form it takes.

My aim is to encourage peace and happiness everywhere … in my family, community, and country, and this includes working toward eliminating any stigma attached to mental health. I trust my story will inspire you to do the same.

THE COMFORTING
SOUND OF SILENCE
By Leah Roncesvalles

For the first time since my diagnosis, I felt hope.

Growing up, I was a perfectionist. I worked hard at school and often stayed up late studying. I could become stressed out very easily, but never thought that one day my perfectionism would take a toll on my mental health.

My story starts in the summer of 2006, my third year of university. Majoring in Math and Statistics, I'd just finished my exams and felt confident I had aced them. Recently hired for a summer office job on campus, I'd also been hired part-time at a marketing company. To top it off, I was about to go on a date with this dream guy I had just met. Everything was going my way. I felt invincible.

Unbeknownst to me, despite the positive events of that summer, I slowly started believing I was on earth for a higher purpose. I felt as though I could see mathematical connections everywhere, even where there were none. For example, numbers on a car license plate would jump out at me and I would connect them to something significant in my life. I believed I was meant to be a leader, maybe the next Einstein or Descartes. I lost all concept of time, and consumed with racing thoughts, I wasn't eating or sleeping.

The day was May 12, 2006. The department I worked for sent me to deliver something to the university president's office. It seemed obvious I was meant to meet the president because I was someone great. However, that day I never returned to work, and just fell off the grid. I wandered the campus aimlessly, knowing I was experiencing something abnormal.

Finally someone noticed I was missing, and the university's health centre reached me on my cell and managed to direct me to the clinic. My memories are foggy, but I recall riding to the hospital in the back of a police car. Upon arrival, I was admitted to the emergency psychiatric ward.

Initially, I was placed in a small room with no windows and a tiny bed. I was very scared. I'll always remember how alone and confused I felt, a state which persisted for a long time. I just wanted to go to sleep and hopefully awaken to some kind of normalcy, but my mind refused to slow down, so slumber eluded me. I recall praying the "Our Father" and when I finished, I realized for the first time how silent my room was, except for the sound seeping through the doorway of someone snoring. Oddly, hearing this sound calmed me down. It reminded me of my grandmother's comforting snore when I slept with her as a child on nights when I was afraid. She passed away in my first year of university, but at that moment I could feel her presence. I knew she was watching over me and would keep me safe. Eventually I drifted off to sleep.

I awoke in a regular hospital room, with my parents and older sister standing by. When I met my hospital psychiatrist initially, she told me that I was diagnosed with bipolar disorder. At this time I was still not well and asked, "Is there medication you could prescribe to make me better?" She replied with, "Leah, bipolar disorder is a life-long condition for which there's no cure." I persisted. "But is there medication I can take?" She answered, "You'll probably be on medication for the rest of your life."

The weight of my diagnosis was suffocating. I didn't even understand exactly what bipolar disorder meant, nor totally believed that I was bipolar. I worried that I wouldn't be the *normal* Leah again. Later that day, a nurse noticed I was having a hard time accepting what had just transpired. Compassionately, she sat down with me to further explain this condition, then even printed out a list of famous people who were bipolar too. She said, "See Leah, one day you will be someone great too!" For the first time since my diagnosis, I felt hope.

I stayed in the hospital for a few weeks, and met many unique people during this period. One morning a guy came into the hospital in a rage and appeared quite violent. He threw a chair at a hospital worker, and was pretty scary. His name was Mark. It turned out he wasn't really all that bad and we became friends. One day, my sister brought me yellow daisies, but within a week or so the daisies started to wilt, so I proceeded to discard them. Mark wanted to keep them. He said, "They'll never die."

Over time, I'd see a yellow daisy pop up here and there, and it made me happy to see one. I saw Mark give one to another patient walking down the hall, and even glimpsed one outside in the peace garden sticking out of the soil. I knew it was from Mark.

Once discharged, I made the decision to return to university to finish my last year. As a high achiever, I thought I could handle a full course load, but it was extremely difficult. For the first time, I was in danger of failing classes, something I'd never done! Depressed about what had occurred, I began to feel sorry for my lot in life; coping and accepting my diagnosis was terribly challenging.

Walking down the street one day after leaving my psychiatrist's office, I felt I'd hit rock bottom and suicidal thoughts filled my head. As I walked past an elderly lady slowly making her way with a walker just like my Grandma's, she smiled. Her smile was contagious and made me smile for the first time in ages. Through that lady, I experienced my Grandma speaking to me, and this became a critical turning point in my recovery. I truly felt the strength of God and had faith I would get through this.

After leaving the hospital, I was placed in an outpatient program and developed a wellness recovery action plan for myself. Family, friends, and health care professionals provided a tremendous amount of support and care. I prayed often and felt my grandmother with me during times I was tempted to give up. I lightened my load by taking some summer courses. I'd graduate one semester later than my classmates but that was okay. I took good care of my health, and went on to complete a Bachelor of Education in Math and Economics. I'm currently teaching high school math and love every day I spend in the classroom. I hope to make meaningful changes by being a good leader and role model, and my passion is to make a difference in the lives of youth in our community.

My manic episode, hospital experiences, and my recovery journey taught me so much. Fear of acceptance, of people's judgments, and fear of being different still exist, but I've learned to have faith in times of despair.

When life seems tough, remember you are not alone. If you're fortunate to have family and friends like I have, they will get you through anything. I sincerely love and respect my parents and it's my intention to always be there for them as they were for me. I will strive to keep the doors of communication open, and make every effort to not get so caught up in busyness that we can't keep in touch.

Most importantly, I realized that overcoming a challenge allows you to become a stronger person. With my newfound strength and resolve, I want to spread awareness and promote a healthy view of mental illness, so that we address these issues as seriously and respectfully as we do our physical problems.

My journey isn't over. I'm still recovering every day. Today, I view what I've undergone as a gift to share. I currently participate in public speaking engagements about mental health and share my experiences. I enjoy doing it to help others and feel I can make a difference even if it's with just one person. Sharing my story is part of my recovery. It nourishes me. My story is who I am.

NEW BEGINNINGS
By Kristen Feasby

At some point in the future,
my goal would be to write a book.

*M*oment by moment … this is how I live my life. I crave hopefulness and happiness for the future. I have come to love each moment of bliss that comes my way, lounging in the warmth of sunshine, smiling when thinking of a friend. I've learned to have gratitude for all things, both large and small. I treasure the little moments and my whole day seems brighter.

In contrast, this is not how I had previously led my life. Depression. Drugs. Anxiety. Addiction. Personality Disorders. Schizoaffective Disorder … all of these illnesses ruled my life with an iron fist.

For fourteen years, I struggled at the bottom of a dark pit. Light would poke holes, letting me know there was still light, and hope.

For me, the first step in my recovery process was acknowledging that I had an addiction and that I did actually suffer from mental illness.

Next, I followed all the steps that individuals take with diagnoses similar to mine:

Psychiatrist ✓

Therapist ✓

Depression Support Group ✓

Lodging in a group home ✓

Meds ✓

Intense In-House Program ✓

After completing the necessary steps, I thought I had recovered. Yeah! Was I wrong! Medications kept changing. I was hospitalized too many times to count. I switched therapists, and even took a Dialectical Behaviour Therapy (DBT) course. Nothing seemed to help. In addition to all of this, I hated the group home I lived in.

A major turning point in my life was realizing how reckless I was. I am in recovery from drug addiction. Each day, I find it hard not to spend crazily, eat outrageous amounts of food, or binge on anything I can get my hands on. I'm in recovery, but the tidal waves keep trying to pull me under. It's definitely an uphill battle at times.

My move to a new group home saved my life! It was at Queenview Residential where I felt myself begin to blossom. There, I found not only a place to live, but I also gained friends and a new family. At Queenview, my life expanded with new activities of daily living and my social life exploded.

I enjoy cooking and baking, exercising and swimming, bowling, shopping, movie night, a social recreation program, and a social night full of friends, music, and dancing. Also offered is an in-house craft program three days a week.

I am so grateful for the staff at Queenview. They have encouraged me to face my challenges head on. It was through this new group home that I was introduced to the Community Connections Program of the Canadian Mental Health Association (CMHA), Aurora. I have learned that connecting to community is a wonderful feeling. Everyone benefits. I love my friends at CMHA, who are a big part of my life.

I've stumbled often, but was fortunate to be lifted up many times by caring individuals who have always been there for me, including my family, and those at Queenview and CMHA. Along with my psychiatrist and therapist, this is the most influential group of people who have helped me to see myself in a new light. When I needed tough love, they were always present.

Looking back, I'm truly humbled by much of my history. I realize now how much stronger I am mentally and emotionally for all that I have been through and continue to live with.

Today, I have learned to live in the moment, no longer dwelling on the past. I've worked hard to get to where I am today—I am in Recovery! I teach a Creative Expressions course at CMHA, Aurora and I love it immensely. I am often impressed by the differences, the happiness, and the smiles that I see on the faces of people around me, when I go to the drop-in at Aurora CMHA. I would be interested in participating more regularly. I'd also like to use my educational background as a Social Service Worker to help make a difference as well.

Most importantly, I have learned to honour myself for who I am, and my unique experience. We all deserve to be respected, by ourselves and others at all times.

At some point in the future my goal would be to write a book where I could share my story in greater length.

And for my family ... that's simple! My goal is to slowly untie the complicated knots and keep working on my relationships. I am more successful now at understanding where people are coming from, and the ability to meet them half way along the relational path is the best thing that has come out of my journey through mental illness.

Last but not least, it's important that I continue to have the courage to stand up and be proud of myself! I recognize that I'm simply a work in progress, but aren't we all?

WHAT WOULD YOU THINK IF?
By Julie Combdon

I wish I could take away his fear ...

W hat would you THINK if:
Your son called from college, four hours away, claiming people were walking on the roof of his apartment building and he could hear them talking about him?

Or ... He told you about the Illuminati and the Canadian Security Intelligence Service (CSIS)? These are now some of the new words in your vocabulary. He calls CSIS on a regular basis, and asks them to send protection from the Illuminati.

What would you DO if:
Your son phoned to request $5,000 to clear a credit card bill, hoping to have a new beginning? It is money you do not have, after already investing $5,000 into

another one of his cards; and the next day, he takes a $5,000 advance out on that same credit card.

Where would you GO if:

Your son informed you he had to move from his place by midnight because he was evicted? He is overwhelmed with constant paranoia that people are drugging his food, knocking him out, and stealing his money. Doors are being locked, windows are blacked out, and the landlord is living on egg shells. His unjustified fear of the police complicates matters.

Who would you CALL if:

Your son called from his phone to say he had to throw away his $700 cell phone because it's been tapped, and people are following him and want to shoot him?

Or … He is in a psychotic state and raging with paranoia so much so that you feel compelled to contact the police to come and calm him, in spite of his fear and your worry? And the police arrive to discover that he is wearing a bulletproof vest and a tape recorder.

Who would you TURN to if:

Your son called you from Niagara Falls saying he tried to leave the country but ran out of gas, and customs agents turned him back? He is now stranded a hundred miles away in the middle of the work day.

What would you DO if:

Your son was released from hospital, transported to a group home forty miles away, and within twenty-four hours he is kicked out?

Or ... He moved twenty-two times in four years and was hospitalized seven times?

HOW would you FEEL if:

Your son called you from a bridge overlooking the highway at 3:00 a.m., and said he could fly but doesn't know how he got there?

Or ... He admits one day, "Mom, I am ready to go to the hospital. Will they help me?"

This is Anthony, who at the time was eighteen, and eleven years later is still suffering from paranoia and schizophrenia with a substance abuse disorder.

With a diagnosis of mental illness, families are in a state of turmoil, not knowing where to go, who to see, what questions to ask, or even what to think, because all the hopes, dreams, and wishes for their loved one are gone. Their quality of life and survival is now in question, and the future is a huge challenge. The profound feelings of grieving and loss are on par with that of a death in the family.

Anthony's parents didn't know where to turn, yet started with some addiction supports, eventually being referred to the Canadian Mental Health Association (CMHA) Family Caregiver Education program.

This ten-week program provided the much needed support for families and caregivers of loved ones with mental illness, along with the help to understand the importance of self-care. It also connected them with resources such as Community Crisis Response Service 310-COPE, addiction services, housing, Ontario Disability Support Program (ODSP), prescriptions, and legal matters. Most importantly, it gave them HOPE ... that things would get better.

After graduating from the program, caregivers are invited to a bi-monthly support group meeting to share any challenges they may be facing, or simply support others in need.

This program gave Anthony's parents HOPE, resources, and a safe place while they went through their journey, and it continues to empower caregivers to advocate for their loved ones with a mental illness.

What would it be like if we didn't have the Canadian Mental Health Association Family Caregiver Education Program, and the support program? We wouldn't know:

- where to turn to
- how to deal with psychosis
- the importance of the Ontario Disability Support Program (ODSP)
- that we are not alone
- how important our self-care is
- … And that there is HOPE

The opportunity to make a difference in the Canadian Mental Health Association community has not only changed the lives of caregivers, but has profoundly changed mine. I am Anthony's mother.

As a business owner, mother, caregiver, and volunteer with the Canadian Mental Health Association, my strength now comes from our Family Caregiver Support Group here in York Region. The past four years, I've found my role as a facilitator in this program and the support group very fulfilling. CMHA, through this service alone, educates approximately seventy-five families each year and aims to do increasingly more.

We are often asked how Anthony is doing now. Well ...

- We don't receive demanding phone calls every day.
- He gets in touch to ask if we can go food shopping together.
- He is able to manage his money on a weekly basis.
- He lets the sun shine in through his windows.
- He is taking his medication most of the time.
- He keeps asking how much longer he can stay at this location.

I wish I could take away his fear of moving for the twenty-third time. He loves where he is; however, its financial burden on us has led me to work six to seven days a week, as ODSP isn't sufficient to support someone with a mental health disorder.

The challenges of finding supportive housing to help someone with paranoia and schizophrenia include:

- Their difficulty in being around lots of people
- Their inability to be in a dark, cold basement
- Their need to be close to family support
- Finding a rental space within the amount that ODSP allows is extremely challenging

We try to look after his basic needs of being safe and warm, fed and dry, and always remain hopeful about what tomorrow will bring.

We continue to give him the supportive housing he needs, with hope that one day he will be approved for the Vulnerable Incentive Program. This is where Anthony is at on his journey, with a positive distance between his teen years and today, and we look forward to a future full of possibilities.

MY JOURNEY TO WHOLENESS
By Susan Callon

Newfound self-esteem, self-respect,
and self-love have emerged from the rubble.

*M*y downward spiral started shortly after an injury
at work. I had slipped and dislocated my
shoulder. The muscles and ligaments were torn. Three
surgeries later, and many challenges with The
Workplace Safety Insurance Board (WSIB), I was
anxious and frustrated, and so began my descent into a
deep depression.

One evening my husband said, "Let's go out for a
drink." This didn't happen very often, so I thought it
was a super idea. I was feeling down and time together
one on one sounded great. I was thoroughly enjoying
the night, until my husband said, "Susan, I've spent

thirty-five years with you but" … the big 'but' … "I don't want another thirty-five years with you."

BAM! I never saw it coming, and my first response was to suggest counseling! "No! I have made my decision," he said. Initially I thought, of course I don't want to be with someone if they don't want to be with me. Was that my stubbornness and defiance taking control as a true-blue Taurus? My mind spun, and in that instant, life changed forever.

My biggest fear was losing my life's dream of having a happy caring family … my fifteen-year-old daughter and a husband that I really did love. Next, I wondered where would I live now, and would I be able to survive on my own? In an impenetrable fog, and not knowing what lay ahead for me, I ended up at Markham Stouffville Hospital (MSH) in the mental health ward.

While I was there, my treatment consisted of patient group therapy recommended by my psychiatrist. Reluctantly I attended all the sessions. Once done with that stage of my recovery, the next step involved outpatient groups through Canadian Mental Health Association (CMHA). This meant more groups! It was definitely a long and tedious fight.

Then one day a nurse, Margie from MSH, was offering a workshop in making sock monkeys. Aha! It struck a chord with me. When I was a young child, an aunt had sent me a beautiful handmade sock monkey for Christmas. I'd always wondered how this lovely gift was made, and now here was my chance to find out. When I went to the workshop, I discovered that it didn't take just one sock; it actually took two. My mystery was solved. I was hooked, and in for the long haul.

Learning this craft ended up being a great tool that helped me to focus in other areas. After mastering the technique, it led me to volunteering and eventually teaching the sock monkey workshop. I then went one step further, and started my own business, Susan Monkey Business, one huge foot into the so-called real world. Sure I still had my ups and downs, but I made sure that I had my other foot firmly planted in the door to CMHA and MSH. They both consistently provided me with great peer support, and the Bridge Program at MSH was immensely helpful in getting me turned around in the right direction.

Eight years later at the age of sixty, and after many extremely helpful programs, I've come to realize that the main drift of everything is being sure that I take care of *myself*. Sometimes this strong-willed, stubborn woman did not want to be there for *herself*, but CMHA always was. I trust that, as I continue to learn about mental health, I will be able to educate others. Currently I speak as part of the CMHA Speakers' Bureau, in an effort to bring more awareness to our community.

The most difficult part of this journey has been letting go of the deep sadness and hateful feelings, but I persevere. And newfound self-esteem, self-respect, and self-love have emerged from the rubble. Needless to say, I'm thoroughly enjoying my new independence.

Six decades, and I'm still here fighting all my fears, new and old. Moving forward, I bravely took the next leap into life's adventure. To help me on my journey financially, I went to my bank … Cash on the line … New car, and an expanded social life. I'm worth it. Everyone is! So take care of *yourself*.

THE DAY MY LIFE CHANGED
By *Charlene Charles*

I have learned how strong and determined I really am.

At twenty-nine years old, I was celebrating becoming an aunt for the very first time. My niece had been born just nine months prior, and I was simply thrilled. Eventually though, the excitement slowly began to fade away and sadness and anxiety overwhelmed me. So many emotions ... I felt worthless and defeated. I would think to myself, I don't fit in anywhere. What's wrong with me? I had no hope and my self-esteem was very low. I hated who I was.

A few months earlier, the dark moments had started to intensify. I didn't want to be around anyone and spent most of my time secluded in my room. The negative thoughts were getting extremely bad, and my anxiety increased noticeably, giving way to panic attacks. I was constantly crying and feeling very, very, very sad, not understanding what was going on or why I was experiencing this. It was getting harder to cope with life and everything else that was going on. I started having thoughts of wanting to hurt myself. I'd look at my niece, this little baby who I loved with all of my heart, and would think how I didn't deserve to have her in my life. I'd tell myself that I needed to protect her from *me,* and began to feel like everyone would be better off if I wasn't around. As each day passed, the vicious cycle grew.

The turning point in my life came on June 5, 2007. I woke up and got ready to go to work as usual. When I arrived though, I went into the bathroom and took half a bottle of Tylenol. I passed out and when I awoke, the paramedics were there. Initially diagnosed with depression and anxiety, this first day of my journey toward healing would teach me who I was, and change my life forever.

I was taken to Markham Stouffville Hospital, and admitted to the psychiatric ward. I met my psychiatrist the next day, and remember feeling very scared following the initial meeting with him. After being hospitalized for three weeks, my diagnosis included depression, post-traumatic stress disorder, anxiety, and borderline personality disorder. Once discharged, I started the

Bridge Program which was the hospital's mental health day program. They and the Canadian Mental Health Association taught me that who I am is okay, and that I'm an amazing woman with a lot to give.

Eight and a half years later, I can thankfully say things have improved significantly. Don't get me wrong; I still have difficult days, but there are fewer of them. Looking back, I have come a long way. I'm now a student at Centennial College in the Community Development Work program. I have been living on my own for five years, and my confidence is growing. I have learned how strong and determined I really am, and have become an advocate for mental health. For the first time in my life, I also have hope, which is a phenomenal feeling.

In the future, I want to be able to give back to my community and help reduce the stigma attached to mental health issues. It would be beneficial to have more programs to assist people dealing with mental illness, and my goal is to do this through the community development work program I'm enrolled in at Centennial College. Education gives us knowledge that can enable people to better understand, thereby decreasing the judgmental attitudes that still exist today. It's my hope that my niece and nephew will grow up to be informed, involved, and compassionate people who can also make a difference.

The most remarkable result that has come from my journey is being able to believe in myself and liking who I am. I'm an amazing person. Mental illness is a battle that I have to fight every day, but I can do it. If I had one thing to share, my message would be to never give up. I definitely won't give up on me.

STEPPING UP
By Gordon Combdon

Change and adaptability are human kind's
greatest tools of survival, yet we resist …

*B*eing a stepparent means to step up! … Step up
and help support the family as a whole, and in my
case, to face the challenges of a child with mental illness.
All too often, I hear about uninvolved stepparents
missing the opportunity to support their spouse and
family. This makes the stepparent part of the problem,
rather than part of the solution; and, in my opinion, it's
the wrong choice to make.

Struggling with rejection from the child is not
uncommon. However, we can still be supportive behind
the scenes. They put rudders on the back of a ship for a
reason … it's a very effective way of guiding a large vessel.
Oddly enough, it works quite well in a family setting also.

Stepparenting can play a critical role in the survival of the family. It isn't easy, but we can help to make it easier for all involved. We can be the calm in the midst of the storm that mental illness creates in a household.

So that my wife, Julie, doesn't need to worry about me or what I am thinking, I have always told her, "Go and do what you need to do to help your son and don't worry about what I may think or how I will react. I will support you both, however things may go, right, wrong, or otherwise. We can always fix it later."

Our best defense as a stepparent is empathy, compassion, unconditional forgiveness, and love, as well as educating ourselves about mental illnesses. Families as a whole must realize that they are dealing with an illness more so than the child, and that the child is struggling immensely too. Education is the key in understanding and responding in every situation; in fact, it's as important to know what not to say as it is what to say.

Prior to our son's mental illness diagnosis, my wife and I thought we were dealing with a relatively normal, frustrated teenage male with a possible addiction issue that we could not figure out. There was a lot of anger within our house and within myself due to respect issues. Nothing we tried seemed to be working, and we constantly tiptoed around situations. Things started to make more sense when we finally did get a diagnosis of paranoia and schizophrenia with a substance abuse disorder. My anger toward our son melted away because I knew this was not him, but a disease we were dealing with.

We began educating ourselves by attending the Family Education Caregivers course put on by the Canadian Mental Health Association (CMHA) and attending the resulting support group. Dealing with the loss of hopes and dreams we'd had for our son and ourselves was debilitating at best, but reading and researching about mental illness has been a huge leap forward in helping us cope with the chaos in our lives.

Change and adaptability are human kind's greatest tools of survival, yet we *resist* change because we often view it as a loss. When one door closes though, another always opens. Resistance is a form of control which we learn at a very young age. Because we cannot compete with adults intellectually, emotionally, or physically, we dig in and resist. This resistance becomes a tool both we and those with a mental illness use to get what they want. It's an illusion of control we all hang on to.

So, as a result of the pain my wife and I experienced, we have accepted a new reality, one of educating ourselves and going with the flow of the day. It is what it is … a new journey of learning and hope. We now volunteer with CMHA, and Julie is one of the facilitators of the Family Education Caregivers group and the Family Education Support group. I co-facilitate this latter group as well as the Support for Depression group. Having experience in these areas has allowed us to help others face the challenges and navigate the systems they will encounter along the way.

Keeping the dream alive for yourselves and your loved one is crucial. Here's an example of one of the things we did. Not long after our son was released from a hospital stay, he announced that he wanted a car, in spite of the fact that the doctor had had his driver's license revoked. We really resisted this proclamation, at first. Upon reconsidering, we thought if he was having a bad time at some point, he could at least go out to the driveway and dream of the day he would regain his freedom. Looking to the future, we decided to keep the dream alive! We bit the bullet and bought the car. That was several years ago and he now has the car, his license, and the freedom that those things represented. This remains a source of pride and achievement he maintains to this day. Being a car guy myself, I certainly can relate.

People say, "Things happen for a reason." I hasten to add, "We give things purpose." If you are wondering where my attitude comes from, I would have to say my parents. I recall them always going out of their way to help people, some of whom they didn't even know. So I asked my Dad one day, "Why do you do all these things for people you don't even know?" He looked at me, smiled, and said, "Because there is no one else to do it!" Damn, that sure stuck with me.

So how is the relationship between my stepson and myself now? It's not as good as it could be, as the tools he employs to maintain a feeling of strength and control still divide and conquer. However, I'm okay with that because it's the illness that compels him. I know that and don't take it personally because it is not about me. I continue to recall the good times we had before his illness, including teaching him how to drive a racing kart, going to car shows, and building things he loved. He still relies on me when he needs something car-related.

Deep down I know he does trust me and I believe things will be better one day. As my Mom used to always say, "Everything always works out for the better." ... smart lady.

So practice self-care. Continue to do things you enjoy doing for yourself. Find a reason to laugh, every day. If you are on this journey as well, I would encourage you to attend support groups, as they are an awesome resource of information and hope. Be aware of your own mental health.

And pick your moments. Along that vein, I'd like to leave you with this thought:

"A smart person knows what to say; a wise person knows when to say it."

Let's step up.

LIFE IS NOT FAIR
By Tylena Perry

I may have lost some battles,
but the war is not over.
I am not going to give up.

*A*t the tender age of five, I was diagnosed with a hearing impairment. Initially, a speech therapist would come to school to work with me, but as I grew older, the way I spoke and my hearing aids accessories attracted continual bullying by the other students. Wires dangling down both ends of my hearing aids fed into an FM system box in order for me to hear the teacher, while he or she would wear a microphone. The temptation of tugging on the wires was too much.

As the children went for recess each day, I'd find reasons to stay inside to avoid being tormented. I volunteered my citizenship in a classroom with handicapped children in wheelchairs with no form of communication and unable to care for themselves, so I'd simply play games on the computer beside them. During lunch, I would go without until I got home from school or hide in the bathroom to eat, but grade eight kids would even kick in my bathroom door. My cultural background dictated that my food was different than what other kids were used to, so they would criticize and say that it smelled bad; meanwhile it was just rice and chicken. How could they be so mean? Things progressed to such a point that I became anorexic, and teachers were quite concerned. They would send me home for my eyes being yellow, assuming I had mono or jaundice. My self-esteem spiraled downward, unimpeded by the fact that I was also battling the effects of abuse.

Throughout most of my life, I carried with me a dark secret that only my sister and a few friends knew about. My sister and I were sexually assaulted at a very young age. Feeling ashamed, we were too frightened to speak to anyone about it, and also felt no one would believe us. We had no support and were afraid of the consequences should we talk about our horrible experience.

It finally took my sister's breakdown and a guidance counselor who informed the authorities, and in 2008, my sister and I were called in to provide statements. That's when we decided to open up about what we had been going through, and not long after, we went to court. We dealt with this whole process for many years, as the court case kept getting adjourned and dragged on for quite a while.

By the time we were actually taking this to trial, I had become pregnant with my first child in October of 2010. At this point, I was not in a very stable position; with no place to live, I was in and out of shelters. I had virtually no family support and feared for my unborn child. All the stress I was dealing with had been building up inside. I used to be able to cope with stress well. Even when I was pressured so much to terminate my pregnancy, I decided to hold my ground. This was a miracle that was ready to happen. I was meant to have this child. God had a plan for me. When I was about six months pregnant, the baby's father deserted me, leaving me feeling abandoned and unloved while I carried his precious child.

June 13, 2011 was the day that I was supposed to have a check-up with my obstetrician. I was in so much pain at the time, but had no idea what was going on. It turned out to be early labour, so the doctor sent me to the birthing ward where I was examined and measured at 1.5 cm dilated. As the original hospital I was scheduled to give birth at did not have the proper care in place, I was transferred to Orillia's Soldier's Memorial Hospital where I was held for a week.

The whole time I was there, my contractions continued, and I made the labour trip all alone. Walking down the halls using my IV pole partner to pace back and forth, and seeing other mothers with their husbands to lean on for support, was the most depressing moment of my life. They would pass by me asking when the baby was coming. They also asked me where the father of the child was. I had no idea how to answer those questions.

My mucous plug did not break until June 16. In the early hours, around 5:00 a.m., I woke to my water breaking. It wasn't until four days later, on Sunday, June 19, that my son was welcomed into the world. Although my mother and I were having some issues with each other, I'm thankful that she was there for my son's delivery. His father did not make an appearance. Born almost a month prematurely from his July 14 due date, and with breathing complications, my little guy was rushed to the Newborn Intensive Care Unit after I held him for just ten seconds. There he stayed for the first week of his life, until he was strong enough to breathe on his own and feed properly. I was so overwhelmed with joy! Obviously I couldn't wait to take him home to show him off to my friends and a few family members.

However, one day while my sweet baby boy slept in the NICU, I headed down to the hospital's gift shop to browse around. I picked out some items that I wanted to purchase, but when I went to pay for them, my bank card transaction was declined. I began to get anxious and started to stress and panic. I did not want to be late going back to breastfeed my baby, so I went to speak to the lady at the switchboard in the lobby. The next thing I remembered was screaming in pain at the top of my lungs. "Help me! Help me! Someone please help me!"

Paramedics ran to my rescue and then I blacked out. I believe I had a minor panic attack. I recall waking up in an emergency room with an IV in my hand. I had no clue where I was, or what I was doing. I felt drugged up, and was acting out and misbehaving. I began crying like a baby, rocking back and forth and talking to myself. There was nothing there. Boom! I blacked out again. I'm not sure how long I remained in a deep sleep, but when I finally woke up, I was being carried by three paramedics, and two nurses. I was restrained, and started kicking and yelling, "No! Let me go! I'm not going to jail! I didn't do anything wrong! Those guys are bad guys." I was horrified to be around the men. I thought they were putting me in a cell; at least that's what it looked like. They slammed me down to the ground and stuck a needle in the fat of my butt to calm me down and put me to sleep. I lost my sense of reality.

I came to in a dark empty space except for a small mattress, a tiny window that couldn't be opened, and a camera in the corner of the room. I started climbing the bed, and dancing around my room. The nurses told me to knock it off because I was acting like I was drunk. The incident felt like what I would perceive to be a paranormal experience. I was hearing voices, hearing demons laughing. I was hallucinating. I had some flash-backs to the time when I was very young, and started crying, terrified to leave my room. I felt like someone was coming for me. I wouldn't go to the washroom because the sound of the toilet flushing scared me. This fear kept me from showering for a whole week! I had no idea that I was locked up in a psych ward. A form was completed to initiate my stay in the hospital until I was properly assessed. Afterward, a psychiatrist explained that I had been diagnosed with postpartum psychosis. What in the world did that mean? I thought. I'd never heard of such a diagnosis or such mental illness before.

A week after I had been detained in the psych ward, I received a shocking phone call. A society worker had called to inform me that my son had been placed in a home, following his discharge from the NICU. The worker mentioned she could not get in touch with anyone and had asked my son's father if he was able to take the baby until I got well. Unfortunately, he told her that he was not in a position to care for a child full time. This hit me like a ton of bricks. I felt as though my child had been abandoned, which was definitely not my intention.

The psychiatrist had prescribed an antipsychotic medication and a mood stabilizer for me. I started to recover over time and was finally discharged after three months. The medications sedated me slightly, but they worked. I was referred to the Early Psychosis Intervention team, and had an amazing worker who helped me immensely. I got involved in a transitional housing program, and sought support from as many organizations as possible, although I was still anxious about reaching out for assistance. I thought I was the only one that had this diagnosis, but of course I was wrong. As each day passed, I continued to struggle with the grief of losing my son. I worked with the Children's Aid Society in an effort to get my child returned into my care. It was the toughest moment of my life because I still lacked family support. I sacrificed my life and put myself in jeopardy to get my child back.

For three years, I was in and out of hospital. I worked with many psychiatrists who all prescribed different medications and who all gave me a different diagnosis. In 2011, I was hospitalized for two years, and it was the most horrible hospital I had ever been to! When I would refuse to take my medications, the nurses would literally shove the medications down my mouth. What the heck kind of treatment is that? I thought. There were times when I got locked up in the "bubble room" for not taking my meds or for acting up.

I disliked the fact that the only solution to everything was medication. Why couldn't they have a counselor come in just to talk instead of always reaching for meds to solve the problem? Never in my life had I thought I would be dependent on medication for the rest of my life. I didn't want to be labeled as a pill popper. Often I was switched to different medications that had various side effects; it was one pill after another. My body began to act funny. Shaking uncontrollably, I couldn't write properly and also developed restless legs. I was taken off all medications and prescribed a Risperdal shot.

On one occasion, I went on a weekend pass and had an extremely bad reaction. Everyone thought I was trying to harm myself. I was taken back to the hospital where they discovered I had developed Neuroleptic Malignant Syndrome, a severe reaction to the shot. I was taken off all medications again, and went through a phase of catatonia where your mind basically shuts down. It's like you're there but you're not ... I stopped eating and talking. I didn't know where I was or what I was doing. I resembled a walking zombie. Seriously! I was drooling everywhere! It wasn't my fault that I stopped caring for myself. I had lost control.

There were a few times my family almost lost me ... I was a vegetable. They never thought they would see a bubbly, happy-go-lucky, intelligent girl in this state. When my sister and my father received the news that the psychiatrist wanted to send me for shock therapy, they came to my rescue as fast as they could. They put a stop to it and started praying for me. What if they had gone ahead with that process and I died? What if I lost my speech? What if I couldn't live a normal daily life anymore? I couldn't advocate for myself. I was too sick. I was still supposed to give evidence in that court case about our abusive situation, but the Crown discovered I was in the hospital and they dropped the court case because I was deemed too ill to testify.

When I got better, I was so upset and devastated that the case couldn't have been postponed until I was well enough. The son of a b**ch deserves to be locked up and justice should've been served for the awful things he did to my sister and me!

The hospital was in the middle of nowhere, with nothing around, and I was far away from family and friends. At the time of my hospitalization, I had a boyfriend who I believed was so wonderful, but he broke up with me because he felt he would never be able to see me again. I wished that we could've worked it through together. I felt horrible that I was "wasting" his time. In a way I was also thankful though because that gave me the opportunity to focus on my recovery. I started attending different groups like cognitive behaviour therapy, drumming, and many more. In the beginning I was scared to walk through the door, having all eyes on me. I was angry at those who put me in the hospital, but realized they did it because they cared and didn't want anything bad to happen. As I opened up to receive support, my life became a little easier. There were so many resources that I never knew existed!

Meanwhile, my son had been placed in a foster home, a situation I'd heard so much negativity about that it horrified me. Fortunately, I ended up getting along with my son's foster family, where a strong bond started with one little note, and we continued writing back and forth. I had the honour to meet his family and I got to learn a lot about the home that he lived in. That's when I felt good inside and confident that my child was in good hands. It was the most amazing experience ever.

Each time the Children's Aid Society was going to transition my son back to my care, my being hospitalized again blew up the possibility. I ceased to find a purpose for living and there are still times where I hate life. When it went to trial, the judge granted my son to be a ward of the Crown with no access for the purpose of adoption. I appealed the decision, and my social worker fought for me to have access with my son. A few weeks passed when I decided to drop the appeal. My thought was what if I went ahead with the appeal and it turned out that I'd never be able to see my son again? I didn't want to risk that so I dropped the case, and in the end, was able to gain openness to my son.

He's been with the same family since he was a baby. It wasn't what I wanted, but I'm beyond blessed that he's with the same family who loves him as much as they love me. If I was to have children in the future, I still fear they might get taken away because of my mental health history. However, now I know what to expect and I know what to do in order to plan for a family.

To this day, I still don't have a clear explanation as to why I was diagnosed with psychosis or schizo-affective bipolar. I have no clue how it ever came into my life. I still search for answers. All I can understand is that it was a hormonal imbalance and when I had the baby, everything that was built up inside just exploded. Surprisingly, I was told that mental health also has to do with the things that you've experienced in the early parts of your life, and that makes sense to me now. Even my sister suffers from anxiety, post traumatic stress, and depression, and my other siblings also suffer from Attention-Deficit/Hyperactivity Disorder (ADHD) and cognitive behaviour disorders. I know a number of people who have been through a tough life, including abuse, and are now battling mental illness. It does not make you any less of a person.

In fact, if you notice depression in someone or you know someone who is dealing with abuse of any form, offer to help right away perhaps by suggesting they speak with someone about it, because without even knowing it, you may be one step closer to saving their life! We are not alone in this world. Many people actually care. There is nothing to be ashamed about and things do get better.

Today I have been two years hospital-free and also made an effort to quit smoking during my hospital stay! Today, I'm only on one medication which I take each night before bed, and I've been doing so well with it, especially considering I used to flush my pills down the toilet. This is the most amazing result I could have ever hoped for. Now I am at my healthiest shape in life, and have finally landed a job that I've always wanted. It may not be my dream job, but it's a survival job until another opportunity comes along. There is hope for us all, and right now, I'm living my life to the fullest and traveling as much as I can.

In the future, I would love to see schools speak more about mental illness, what it is and how it can affect an individual. There has been much stigma around mental illness, and I'm certain education can help eliminate that. I also want to reach out to children who are dealing with any form of abuse, because those children are the ones who are at greater risk for mental illness. Lastly, I'd also love to reach out to young women to help them implement the right plan of care for when they are ready to start their families, hopefully to avoid the kind of scenario I had.

I am so thankful to my case manager at the Canadian Mental Health Association (CMHA) for hooking me up with the drop-in centre and youth programs. I really like to get out and meet new people and relate to them with the stuff that I've dealt with as well. The people I've met are super incredible. They are such strong and amazing troopers. I may have lost some battles, but the war is not over. I am not going to give up, and neither should you!

KEYS TO SUCCESS
By Leah Bader

*It was up to me to create a better life,
and with help ... I've accomplished many goals.*

Today is a miracle, a very special gift. I've reached numerous difficult milestones throughout my life. That said, I never thought in a million years I could get my story down on paper and have it make total sense. Even more surprising is the fact that I can get up in front of people, and hear my voice as I talk to them about my journey. I was pretty withdrawn before, and now I can talk to everyone—wow. In fact, now it's hard to shut me up. Amazingly, I'm able to socialize as well, and give back in response to what has been given to me ... which is all quite new.

I am the first-born child of a very young couple who weren't ready to be parents, creating a rough and rocky start to life. Unwanted and unloved, I lacked both the physical and emotional nurturing every child needs. Growing up in this cold, critical, and fearful environment led to very low self-esteem, anxiety, and depression. In addition, I was diagnosed early on with a learning disability, which my parents had a hard time accepting and coping with.

Because of my make-up and upbringing, I know I'm predisposed to mental illness. Some of the other challenges I deal with are hand-eye coordination, social problems, trouble with balancing and weight, and being cross-eyed (which thankfully has been fixed). As a result, I was very clumsy and uncoordinated and couldn't do anything well or understand things clearly. I started isolating myself, because I was very insecure and unable to function socially. Told I'd never amount to anything and that I was really dumb and stupid, I began to believe it.

Despite all my sufferings, I was overjoyed when my sisters were born and I became a second mother to them. My first sister was born sixteen months after me, followed by another sister seven years afterward. Finally, one more sister arrived seventeen years later. I was in heaven; despite all my problems, I loved babies. I could only relate to babies and children much younger than me.

However, playing and caring for them ended as they grew and started to change as bullying and fighting became the norm. Hate notes were constantly pushed under my bedroom door. They teased and harassed me so much; I was always in such turmoil. I became enraged, hurt, frustrated, and my anger soon turned to hate. As the oldest, I always got blamed; everything was my fault. Inevitably, the feelings and words were born, they became alive and real ... I was useless, dumb, stupid, fat, and ugly. The harder I tried to overcome, the more I failed.

About this time, a major shift took place and as I reached my teen years, I shut down. In my place stood a marionette puppet with no mind or brain, unable to think or do anything positive. Afraid to be me, I grew worse. In my paralyzed state, my parents tried to shelter me from my fears of anything in life, including myself. At this point in time, I would love to find my public school teacher, who would probably have tears in his eyes and fall to the floor in disbelief, because back then my go-to line was, "I can't do it." I couldn't and wouldn't do anything by myself; I was afraid to step outside my comfort zone, and it would drive him crazy.

In addition, I'd bury all my emotions, refrain from being seen or heard, and avoid any kind of interaction. When I really got upset, which was constant, my thumb was my only comfort and my best friend. I would curl up into the fetal position, hide and cry underneath my blankets, and suck my thumb for hours. As a result, my front teeth shifted forward, and that's when I inherited the name of Bucky the Beaver from my father. Home and school were two traumatic places for me; I hated both intensely.

I wanted to die! I had nothing to look forward to. Now, only fifty-three years later, my life both past and present makes more sense to me. Recently I learned I have chromosomal deletion syndrome; I'm missing chromosome 16, which may be linked to my mental illness. If I haven't experienced everything in life, I feel I've come pretty close, which helps me relate to so many people of all ages. Having experienced all kinds of traumatic abuse and varying forms of bullying about my looks, weight, and intelligence, this neglected, rejected soul came to believe she had been stripped of everything, and she was. Without any physical and emotional love, praise, or acceptance left a shell of a woman with no self respect, self-compassion, or self-esteem; I became vulnerable and gullible, and allowed myself to be violated. I thought if I permitted that behaviour, I would fit in and people would like me. I made stupid choices and decisions without thinking, and didn't care what the consequences were; I just wanted to self soothe and feel better.

I'm ecstatic to say that I've accepted and beaten many odds today, and have raised five successful kids. My first daughter also suffers with mental health concerns and is presently focusing on getting better. My second child is currently completing her PhD in Criminology and Sociology, while my third child works full time at a youth drop-in centre and is also a tattoo artist. My fourth child is completing her Masters in Molecular Medicine and my last child is on the honour role and is teaching herself sign language. I've graduated from college with honours in the P.S.W. program and have achieved a lot in life which I never thought possible.

It's important to be happy, content, satisfied, and proud. It was up to me to create a better life, and with help from the Canadian Mental Health Association (CMHA), Jewish Family Services, and The Women's

Centre, I've accomplished many goals. The keys to success for me are: counseling, a good sense of humour, and a support system with caring people. The qualities I needed to become successful are: hope, self-love and compassion, good attitude, determination, open-mindedness, patience, honesty, perseverance, and creativity.

Do you know the best thing to come out of this journey so far? It's the person I've turned out to be, and also meeting someone very special who has gone through his own rough journey. We've connected, have the same passion and compassion to help and support one another, and have joined together to form a social support group where we can help others as well as ourselves. We love volunteering together and it's helped us both in our recovery. Peers really enjoy our company; they love our association, and so do we. I realize now that it's okay not to have a family, and that you can still flourish with close friends, and professionals such as those I've come to know.

My passion is to always help people and lead them to the right resources. Everyone deserves a chance, and I'm so thankful for the encouragement I've received.

UNIQUELY DISORDERED
By Randee Korman

I danced and sang as if my life
depended upon every move I made.

I have suffered (hate that word), lived, battled, fought with my mental illness since I was child, and I am now fifty-five. It amazes me that I can say this because I never thought I would reach this age. That's a very profound statement. I always thought my mental illness would by now have somehow taken me. I have two suicide attempts under my belt, so to speak, and lurking at the back of my mind, a plan to end my life lies unfinished. At times, this complex mind of mine can be a very dark and scary place to be. So I have to ask myself these questions. Where do I begin? How do I talk about myself without having everything come flooding back and doing damage to my RECOVERY? Yes, RECOVERY.

I believe I was born with mental illness. I believe that because all I remember from my childhood and throughout my life was unhappiness, not having a sense of what it was like to be happy. A child should always have a sense of wonderment, of being carefree and rolling with whatever comes along. That was not me. Darkness, sadness, and feeling like my head was on fire because of all the frenzied thoughts that surrounded me ... that was my world. To this very day what I felt as a child I live with even now. Writing this and memorializing this means I have to beat back the pain.

No friends, hardly any social life to speak of, abusive and destructive relationships, my world was and still is an extremely small one. Trust in other people, and myself, remains in short supply, and I beat myself up pretty good too. Even to this date, my body is often full of bruises that I feel compelled to hide; if anyone saw them, I would somehow have to explain them away. Living a good quality life never appeared to be a possibility, and I sometimes still feel that way.

Along the way I have seen many health professionals. When I was seven and just beginning my school life, the principal at the time called my mother to say he had some real concerns, serious enough to warrant further investigation. During a classroom observation, he had noticed my unusual and distracted behaviour. When the teacher had instructed us to open our math books, I began clearing my desk, and appeared as though I was off in my own little world. Enter The Hospital for Sick Children where I was diagnosed with a learning disability called dyslexia and Mirror Image. In my teen years, another hospitalization resulted in a diagnosis of chronic to acute clinical depression. Much later I was again hospitalized and ultimately diagnosed with bipolar 2, followed by yet another hospital stay where I was reassessed and told I did not have bipolar 2 ... I had Borderline Personality Disorder (BPD) and Body Dismorphic Disorder, and Anorexia Nervosa. "What the hell was that?" I said to myself as I walked out dazed, confused, and totally defeated.

The only words I could think of were mired in muck and damaged. These labels have had a very negative effect on me, and although I've been on a lot of medications in the past, I am now, by choice, drug-free.

I'd like to share one childhood memory that has stayed with me. The one thing I loved to do was descend into the basement and play my records ... actual vinyl records (that's all there was back then). I played them so much I knew every word, and I danced. Oh, how I danced. I made up a lot of my own choreography to all the songs, and became pretty good at lip synching too. I used to pretend that I was on stage entertaining an arena full of people. Basically I escaped.

I danced and sang as if my life depended upon every move I made. To this day I still do it. Self-soothing is what they call it in Dialectical Behavioural Therapy (DBT). This skills program and its facilitator, Glenys Smith Elliott, were definitely positive game changers in my world.

While lives were going on around me, I was in the basement. When Paul Simon wrote, "I Am a Rock," it was as if he was thinking of me when he wrote it. When I first heard those words, the feelings brought out the fact that I continued to have some pretty significant walls around me. These fortress-like walls that I've constructed are my defense. However, these protective walls can also be a double-edged sword because they have prevented me from enjoying a full life.

Considering my beginnings, I can now appreciate how my educational path unfolded. I have honour degrees from not just one, but two colleges. I can interact with people, but it isn't easy. I fight every day to maintain my stability, and constantly battle with my eating disorder. Learning to do things takes me longer. Judgements are a big thing for me ... not only those that I place upon myself, but those of other people. I have lost great portions of my life due to mental illness, but now I am dealing with that loss and finding out that I am uniquely qualified to help others identify their strengths and build upon them, just as I am now building upon mine.

The soothing words from "An American Hymn" (the main theme from the TV miniseries, East of Eden), lyrics by Molly Ann Leiken, music by Lee Holdridge, are so significant to me. I listen to and absorb them whenever thoughts of desperation attempt to invade my turbulent mind.

My perseverance keeps me going. Eventually, I would like to bring my mom and her sisters back together in some way. They all have health challenges and it would be nice for them to overcome their perceived differences. I would like to become a Peer Support facilitator. Hopefully I can complete my training within the very near future. Momentum is the key here.

The most amazing thing that has happened to me on this journey is my involvement with CMHA's Speakers'

Bureau. The people I have met and the speeches I have heard and given have propelled me to a new level, and provided a lot more richness in my life. Thank you, CMHA, for the wonderful opportunities. With people like you, tomorrow is something I can anticipate, because in spite of the fears, I now believe in the possibilities.

Poetry

NATURE AND STUFF
By Patrick Philpott

A quiet forest in a distant land
holds to its purpose and keeps to its plan.
In constant motion and rhythm it moves;
in its wake we follow its clues.

We look down at the trees from towers we built.
We gaze at the heavens with our constructed eye.
The illusional answers eternally drive us,
as we reach through the mist to the distant sky.

Within our sight, but beyond our reach,
if we listen, it can teach
'til it moves again at a timely pace
like the wind, to a distant place.

ICE PLANET
By Patrick Philpott

Ice of many colours, releasing nitrogen gas,
thin atmosphere waxes and wanes.
Snowy planes in frozen mass
are locked in cycles and frosty chains.

Vast arctic landscape, scant seasonal shifts,
brittle earth from weather pattern.
Grey-white wasteland, mountains and rifts
surrounded by rock and stone like Saturn.

Elemental forms, move far from the sun,
drifting through space on solar wind.
Multiple parts, yet floating as one
spin through time, like a curve ball spun.

SUNSHINE
By Stephen Marcus

I have written and spoken long and hard about my past,
of the forces and events which have shaped my world.
My story is not unlike those told by many others.
We can all express a photo of our tales through words.

Within a group there is encouragement to use our voice
and paint a past picture of when our lives were dark;
no sense of any hope, too blind to any sign of sunlight;
no way to access a ladder and climb out of our hole.

We then speak with a strong voice about a turning point,
an arbitrary period in time to which we sharply return.
It's a river which definitely varies with ebbs and flows.
It is a port where our mental challenges began to ease.

I listen carefully to the words used to describe recovery.
We all have our own definitions of what that word means.
The stage of our story where one currently exists
is explored in great detail with an eye to what's next.

For me, recovery tumbles like a waterfall of words and
  phrases.
I write what is heartfelt, crying out deep from within my soul.
The words speak of the pain, darkness, and anguish as a child,
but they are also the vision of the current and the future.

It is these pictures of where I am and where I wish to go.
Positive growth and a strengthened mind is my present.
Clearly seeing the world through my brand new insights,
my head and heart awaken with the cobwebs dusted off.

I like the path before me upon which I lightly tread.
My body confidently tells me it's now set to travel forward.
Heart and mind have packed their bags and goals together;
I'm quite ready to take the show out on the road ahead.

When we are young the world is full of wonder and dreams.
Wherever we look, all that's seen is fresh, bright, and shiny.
There are no boundaries, no fences to contain our world.
Life presents many musical songs as in a chorus of one.

It is here that I now find a joyous feeling like a young child.
Reborn and happy, I look at myself as if I am new.
The world seems secure and safe; the future far away.
I am loading my red wagon, ready for that long anticipated
  trip.

ATMOSPHERIC PRESSURE
By Patrick Philpott

The tops of trees, above thick fog;
the forest floor is shaded.
High-rise buildings amongst the smog
leave the skyline half faded.

Jaded folks walk in their grids –
on city streets like veins.
Trains and rivers carry the kids –
cheap housing, growing pains.

Imagined chains and locked cages
stifle creativity.
We all shine on different stages
with unique ability.

DESTRUCTION / CONSTRUCTION
By Patrick Philpott

Crooked old structures engulfed by flame,
memories up in smoke.
Choking oxygen gives up its claim
to a dark and shaded cloak.

Dust and fire, falling timbers,
stone foundation still remains.
Blackened rock, infernal cinders,
dropping ash, with no sign of rains.

The strains of rebuilding and pains have worth
as dust and ashes return to the earth.
Ill conceived structures have need of destruction
for a fresh plot of land, and clear reconstruction.

BORDERLINE LIFE
By *Julie Everson*

All my pain seems to create a beautiful symphony.
Each note resounds from a scar etched deep in my heart.
Its frailty peeks through from behind sparkling brown eyes
as a women giving up, raises her face to the skies
lamenting, "I don't know if I've ever meant anything to
   this world,
but am I precious to you Lord? Should I still try?"

The horror of all the red Kool Aid when I ripped my
   Play-Doh arms apart,
filled me with such anxious desperation and need.
Became tears all these years later, and I realize the scars
   will always be a part of me;
turns out I wasn't made of pliable Plasticine.
The reality was that God filled that deep need and
   showed pure love to me
and I too would gain my freedom.

The patches of purple and blue left by men's anger,
and I realize I never knew bruises could burrow so deep.
I suffered in silence, scared to be by myself in case he
   were to leave.

The beauty of a smile as friendly strangers paused to say hi;
small moments of joy stood together like soldiers while I
   struggled to get by.
Lives touching for a moment so precious in this busy,
   hurried world.
Worn out shoes shuffle down the street; I felt the financial
   desperation and need.
Wealth as foreign as a homeless person driving a Mercedes.

Most people just want compassion, someone to look at
   them and really see.
Do they glimpse the spectacular person I'm meant to be?
I feel myself reflect the environment around me ...
the broken sidewalks and garbage strewn between trees.
I stood among those whom society left behind,
because I knew the Lord would stand with me.

I put my music on random shuffle; I don't care what plays.
Just sing to me. Lull my racing thoughts into dreams.
I'm sure they never meant to leave ...
a baby inconceivably abandoned into a stranger's arms on a
   busy city street.
Then the beauty of a foster mom who created a blanket—
   made just for me.
With the tenuous strength of experience, I record all that
   has transpired.

HEARTS LINKED BY COURAGE

I was a teen, when my story took this twist.
Hospitalized & diagnosed, I was told this is it—the border.
I'd never grow beyond this point; borderline personality
   disorder ...
borderline between peas and carrots it seems.
Then, blossoming, I grew to encompass this part of me.
Now I can see beauty and humour in life that most others
   can't see.
Making others laugh would become natural for me.

I've learned to deflect judgmental stares like sunshine
   bounces off a lake,
sending a brilliant shimmer of summertime haze.
Sometimes, like a dandelion puff floating in the breeze
   comes an insane urge
to ditch the boxcar of this stalled train and fly off wherever
   the track meanders,
but a safe love has found me and keeps me here and I will
   never leave,
although I yearn to discover things as yet unseen.
Sometimes my heart races and skips a beat.

We're all given these bodies in which to live ...
little vessels to carry our souls and bright eyes to peer out
   from it.

As the world wears us down with its day-to-day problems
   like poverty and public disdain,
we search for things to cling to, so we can alleviate the pain.
People distract us, and they can play cruel games.
I've seen too many lost to drugs ... thinking they've found a
   way to escape,
they really are just cementing their fate. Drugs slowly drain
   your life away.

Can something so precious as a soul be laid to waste? Yes, it
   happens every day.
Once bright lights fade to grey, there is only One who can
   change the outcome.
I know, because out of a pit I was raised.
I'm a survivor of many terrible things, and Jesus poured his
   grace out on me.
In the wake of years of drug abuse, lingering side effects
   steal my breath away.
I thank God for everyday and that He kept me from
   throwing myself away.
Drugs rip so many lives to shreds;
I know I can stand though, as long as old habits aren't
   nurtured.

I remember back to sixth grade—I couldn't focus or keep
   quiet, then finally
the teacher stopped and turned to me.
He said, "Everyone is listening; tell them what you need to
   say."
I knew I should say something monumental to the world;
instead I said nothing and willed everyone to just look away.

Have you ever been so broke you had to use a voucher to
   get clothes and a coat?
If you don't have any change they put your things in a
   garbage bag—"those bags cost money."
Walk home with a garbage bag of things from a Goodwill
   store and watch how people stare!
If you saw the stares would you be able not to care?
It's as though poverty is a disease and my garbage bag is a
   label marking me.
It's a good social experiment in the least but also an excuse
   to swim in escapist seas.
Try carrying around a garbage bag full of clothes for a day.
See how many self-righteous stares you can count along
   the way.

Here's my point; I see a lady with all the bling stare up and
   down at me.

I'm tempted to yell at her that she is no better than me.
Her fur coat and jewelry don't raise the value of her soul,
and mine is worth its weight in gold.
Gotta keep it real and not get disillusioned;
it's a material world that beckons and divides reality.
Your shiny car and my dirty streets; social class means
    nothing to me.
Just as hard as another label to create; and as easy as a
    smile to erase

I am mentally ill and so easy to judge and stigmatize.
You say I'm crazy or weird but I say hey, I am different,
and maybe that's just how God wants some people made.
I laugh easier, I cry easier;
I am passionate about rescuing snails from being crushed
    by people's feet …
a terrible fate indeed.

I practice an art of being happy just because I choose to be,
and I try not to stay angry and this encourages my
    sobriety.
Do you think I'm not doing anything with my life because
    I'm on disability?
Maybe you think I am unstable, but I say, "Look how I
    stay on this ball and keep it rolling."

I look at myself and others with mental disabilities and see
   great strength and pain.
I see deep love and child-like faith.

I see humour in things that make me giggle out loud and a
   grin sweeps my face.
I see someone special that a diagnosis can't hold.
So please before you judge me, please try and see my soul.
The horror is that sometimes stigma is worse at home, and
   there is nowhere safe to go.
People who are supposed to love you, make your blood run
   cold.

Yes, I'm no longer frozen; I am free!
So please, when I stand up, listen to me.
When I smile I want it to be more than displaying the cute
   gap in my front teeth.
I want it to resonate from deep inside of me.
The world needs something real and real smiles are lacking
   in our streets ...
Not, "Buy this!" smiles on ads or "Elect Me!" smiles on
   posters stabbed in the grass.
Real smiles have the uncanny ability to make someone
   glad.

So I try to give them when I can, but unfortunately,
so much is fake in the world that most eyes are downcast.

The beauty is I've learned how to let the mean words go.
I turn the pain into art and just let the words flow.
They can't touch me; they can't take hold.
The battle is real; my struggle is real, and here, this smile is
    real too.
I'm opening up my heart just to give it to you as you many
    times did for me.
Can you do the same and smile for me too?
Yes that's me randomly dancing down the street.
What's this body good for if I can't move my feet?
I close my eyes and tap out the beat, tap out the beat inside
    of me.
I think now they will see me.

PERMISSIONS

Every attempt has been made to give proper acknowledgement, and access appropriate permissions for quotes. Any oversights are purely unintentional. In the unlikely event something has been missed, please accept our regrets and apology, and contact us immediately so we can investigate and rectify as needed.

PUBLISHER'S NOTE

As founder of the *Hearts Linked by Courage* series, and contributing author and creator of the first book, I am truly humbled by the belief that CMHA Director of Programs, Neil Howard, and the Speakers' Bureau, had in my vision.

None of us are spared hardships in life. When it comes to mental illness, most of us have been affected in some way, or know of someone who has been gripped with the challenges associated with depression, bipolar, schizophrenia, addiction, and so on.

I have always been moved by those who seem to go through such tragedy and upset in their lives, yet find a way to look at the bright side, such as what they learned, how they grew, and who they helped along their path. This has always motivated me to do the same as much as I possibly can. It's also what contributed to the dream I had for the *Hearts Linked by Courage* series.

Other people's stories move and encourage us. I wanted the *Hearts Linked by Courage* series to echo this message, that we're all in this life together to help one another, and that there is much more to learn and become through the dark times in our lives versus the easy, more predictable times. It's not that we want or wish for those difficult circumstances, but when they're upon us, we have a choice.

The stories from the CMHA York and South Simcoe Speakers' Bureau both educate and inspire, and address the many choices and turning points in each journey. They instil confidence and belief that, no matter the circumstance, we are strong enough to rise above the most challenging situations life can dish out. They have opened their hearts, bared their souls, and bravely revealed to us the light at the end of the tunnel.

Much gratitude also goes to the amazing support Gayle Clarke has given this project and the series as a whole. Her thoughtful assistance throughout the editing process, incredible compassion, and life experience, made a tremendous difference to all involved.

Again, I am indebted to Neil and the story contributors whose words have brought to life the second book in this series. Perhaps they've even sowed the seed and example of how other groups can benefit by using the *Hearts Linked by Courage* series to share their own stories of education and hope.

Sheri Andrunyk
Publisher, Author, Speaker, Mentor
Insightful Communications (I C) Publishing
Committed to Quality Content, Design, and Platform

ICPublishing.ca / ICBookstore.ca